CB078521

Pathway to Grammar

Student's Book

3

Richmond

Richmond
58 St Aldates
Oxford
OX1 1ST
United Kingdom

Pathway to Grammar Student's Book Level 3

First Edition: 2015
Sixth Reprint: February 2020
ISBN: 978-607-06-1082-0

Av. Río Mixcoac No. 274, Col. Acacias,
Benito Juárez, C.P. 03240, Ciudad de México

Publisher: Justine Piekarowicz
Editorial Team: Jennifer S. Li, Joep van der Werff
Art and Design Coordinator: Marisela Pérez
Design: Erika Martínez
Layout: Paola Romero
Pre-Press Coordinator: Daniel Santillán
Pre-Press Team: Susana Alcántara, Virginia Arroyo
Cover Design: Erika Martínez

Cover Photograph: ©**THINKSTOCK:** iStock (Mike_Kiev, VitalyEdush, whitetag); Polka Dot (Jupiterimages)

Illustrations: Erick Arellano pp. 8, 11, 26, 67; Guadalupe Calvo pp. 5, 6, 28, 46, 48, 65, 69; Alejandro Herrerías pp. 7, 9, 27, 47, 51; Diego Llanso pp. 16, 18, 35, 36, 41, 59, 79; Alma Nuñez pp. 15, 38, 56; Sara Palacios pp. 17, 37, 55, 60, 78; Emmanuel Urueta pp. 25, 45, 49, 70; David Yañez pp. 19, 39

Photographs: ©**REPOSITORIO:** Ediciones Santillana, S.A. (Argentina) pp. 18, 36, 50, 58, 74; Editorial Santillana, S.A. (Guatemala) p. 40; Richmond Publishing S.A. de C.V. pp. 13 (Elias Hermann Salas Martínez), 18 (Marcela Gómez Ruenes), 83 (Elias Hermann Salas Martínez); Santillana Educación S.L. pp. 4 (Javier Jaime Sánchez), 16 (STOCK PHOTOS LATIN STOCK), 40, 50 (HighRes Press StockÂ), 63, 74 (Agencia HighRes Press Stock, AbleStock.com); ©**THINKSTOCK:** AbleStock.com pp. 34 (Hemera Technologies), 53 (Hemera Technologies); amana images pp. 44 (amanaimagesRF), 82 (DAJ); BananaStock p. 53 (BananaStock); Blend Images p. 67 (Dave & Les Jacobs); Creatas pp. 14 (Jupiterimages), 16 (Creatas), 21 (Jupiterimages), 33 (Jupiterimages), 54 (Creatas); Design Pics p. 80 (Design Pics); Digital Vision pp. 14 (Thomas Northcut), 15 (Siri Stafford), 32 (Toby Burrows), 44 (Digital Vision), 53 (Bec Parsons), 64 (James Woodson), 66 (Davis McCardle), 73 (Michael Blann), 74 (David Sacks, James Woodson); Fuse pp. 4 (Fuse), 13 (Fuse), 14 (Fuse), 44 (Fuse), 49 (Fuse), 51 (Fuse), 52 (Fuse), 53 (Fuse), 54 (Randy Faris/Fuse), 55 (Fuse), 80 (Fuse); Getty Images News p. 81 (Spencer Platt); Goodshoot p. 74 (Jupiterimages); Hemera pp. 14 (Karl Martin), 23 (Cathy Yeulet), 26 (Ekaterina Perepelova), 27 (Daniil Kirillov), 30 (Aleksandr Ugorenkov), 42 (Ramona Smiers), 58 (Norbert Martin), 59 (Sean Nel, Zeljko Bozic), 67 (Jan Remisiewicz), 74 (Cathy Yeulet), 77 (Cathy Yeulet), 79 (Cathy Yeulet); Ingram Publishing pp. 15 (Ingram Publishing), 21 (Ingram Publishing), 24 (Ingram Publishing), 80 (Ingram Publishing); iStock pp. 3-83 (Ociacia), 3 (julos), 4 (Tatsianama, tupungato), 8 (SergiyN), 8 (justme_yo), 9 (enisaksoy, djcodrin, Bibigon, annata78, ISerg, Serg_Velusceac, AlexRaths, changered), 10 (ahavelaar, spaxiax, Grigoriy Lukyanov, Vladimir Igonin), 12 (Alexander Shirokov, StudioM1, Irantzu_Arbaizagoitia), 13 (Glenda Powers, monticelllo), 14 (david franklin, sjenner13, gangliu10, vladimyr, lisafx, pojoslaw, Tracy Fox), 15 (DanComaniciu, dolgachov, petrdlouhy, videodet), 16 (Mitch Aunger, Thomas Lammeyer, Eric Simard, peterspiro, a_lis), 18 (conejota, Tomwang112), 21 (xerviar, galaxy67, aunaauna, sonia_ai, MojoD, colematt, maxicam), 22 (Hongqi Zhang, McIninch, SergiyN), 23 (cmcderm1, RimDream, Gualtiero Boffi, akekoksomistock), 24 (Robyn Mackenzie, Hyrma, vikif, mofles, Tiramisu Art Studio, nataliaspb, Devonyu, anna1311, aarrows), 25 (joey333, yigitgunel, srdjan111), 26 (Jonas Gunnarsson, VictoriAnna, Marvid), 27 (Nadezhda Bolotina, Наталья Чирцова, Prill Mediendesign & Fotografie, sergoua), 30 (AndreyShtanko, Igor Tarasyuk, cynoclub, karandaev, Piotr Krześlak, damedeeso, prapassong), 31 (OlgaMiltsova, antpkr, Freer Law, Shaiith), 32 (dolgachov), 33 (Jean-Pierre Tilborg, Mike_Kiev, Mike_Kolesnikov, aetb), 34 (Natasa Blagojevic-Stokic, Brent Hofacker, Oleg Saenko, Yuriy Mazur, milanws, McIninch, Smitt, fotocerva), 35 (Sashkinw), 36 (richardschramm, RyanKing999), 42 (James Phelps, JuliA!n Rovagnati, Gines Valera Marin, sashahaltam), 43 (Sashkinw), 44 (Denis Raev, encrier, photochecker, j-wildman), 45 (ARICAN, _human), 46 (Darja Tokranova), 47 (filipe varela, LUNAMARINA, agencyby, andresrimaging), 48 (Robert Pavsic, Scott Griessel), 49 (James Tutor, Rrrainbow, CerebroCreative, VitalyEdush, Shelly Perry), 50 (Iwona Grodzka, agustavop, firstpentuer, Denyshutter, scanrail, onairjiw, metrokom), 51 (Waldemar Dabrowski, GlobalP, WilleeCole, cynoclub, filmfoto), 53 (monkeybusinessimages, OcusFocus), 54 (Elena Elisseeva, Jacob Wackerhausen, geniebird, karandaev, Antonio_Diaz, OSTILL, monkeybusinessimages), 55 (Brad Sauter, Oli_Trolly, BlueOrange Studio, monkeybusinessimages, dolgachov, Neonci), 57 (whitetag, serkorkin, mikemcd), 58 (Daniel Hurst, Jose Gil, Anna Rise, reanas, mg7, Meinzahn), 59 (Pavel Losevsky, Julia Nuttall, foto76, monkeybusinessimages, XiXinXing), 61 (Jan Tyler, MicroWorks, Paffy69), 62 (eikrid), 64 (PrinPrince, swisshippo, Smithore, ewan chesser, Michael Hite, leungchopan, thawats, ahlaphot, 36clicks, Jacob Wackerhausen, kati1313), 65 (Victoire_Lefevre, changered), 66 (mariakbell, ivkuzmin, Houshmand Rabbani, kenDuffney, Joe Belanger), 67 (ttretjak, Jacynth Roode, Eric Isselée, nickp37, AndreaAstes), 68 (Hung_Chung_Chih, studio7, Iryna_Rasko, cowboy5437, Anagramm), 69 (Eric Isselée, GlobalP, Jeremiah Nichols, Anthony Cake), 72 (Hung_Chung_Chih, Eric Isselée, GlobalP), 73 (vencavolrab, bigjom), 74 (PIKSEL, cynoclub, m-imagephotography, Moti Meiri, Willard), 75 (monkeybusinessimages, YasnaTen, colematt, bannerwega, sonia_ai, nebojan), 76 (Mike Sonnenberg), 77 (singlewhitepixel), 79 (IPGGutenbergUKLtd), 81 (redstallion), 82 (Natthawat Wongrat, mandygodbehear, Jacek Chabraszewski), 87 (dolgachov), 88 (Dorottya_Mathe), 91 (studioarz); iStock Editorial pp. 10 (Aneese), 23 (robtek), 24 (Eldad Carin), 50 (ILCphoto); mana images p. 16 (mana images); Monkey Business pp. 13 (Monkey Business Images Ltd), 49 (Monkey Business Images/Stockbroker); moodboard pp. 14 (moodboard), 24 (moodboard), 55 (moodboard), 80 (Mike Watson Images); Photodisc pp. 13 (Photodisc, Amos Morgan, Thomas Northcut), 14 (Siri Stafford), 44 (Keith Brofsky), 47 (Ryan McVay), 54 (Michael Blann, Digital Vision), 62 (James Quigley), 71 (Blue Jean Images), 79 (Barry Austin Photography); PhotoObjects.net pp. 59 (Hemera Technologies), 74 (Hemera Technologies); Photos.com pp. 14 (Jupiterimages), 24 (Jupiterimages), 34 (Jupiterimages), 66 (Jupiterimages); Pixland pp. 12 (Jupiterimages), 24 (Jupiterimages), 54 (Pixland); Polka Dot pp. 34 (Polka Dot Images), 51 (Jupiterimages); Purestock pp. 44 (Purestock), 54 (Purestock); Ron Chapple Studios p. 51 (Ron Chapple Stock); Stockbyte pp. 12 (Stockbyte), 14 (Stockbyte, George Doyle & Ciaran Griffin), 22 (George Doyle), 27 (Stockbyte), 34 (Thinkstock Images, Comstock Images, altrendo images), 36 (Thinkstock Images), 50 (Jupiterimages), 54 (Stockbyte), 59 (Jupiterimages), 76 (Comstock Images), 77 (BrandX Pictures); TongRo Images p. 54 (TongRo Images); Top Photo Group p. 13 (Top Photo Corporation); Valueline p. 24 (Valueline); View Stock p. 10 (View Stock); Wavebreak Media p. 10 (Wavebreakmedia Ltd), 14 (Wavebreakmedia Ltd), 53 (Wavebreakmedia Ltd), 64 (Wavebreakmedia Ltd); Zoonar p. 10 (Zoonar RF), 29 (Zoonar RF)

Printed in Brazil by Forma Certa Gráfica Digital
Lote: 794435
Cod: 292710820

Contents

Unit 1

B C

A

MARCH					
Monday	Tuesday	Wednesday	Thursday	Friday	Saturday / Sunday
27	28	29	30	31	1 / 2

days of the week — weekend

JANUARY				
M	T	W	Th	F
✓	✓	✓	✓	✓

always

APRIL				
M	T	W	Th	F
✓	✓	✓		✓

usually

JULY				
M	T	W	Th	F
	✓		✓	

sometimes

OCTOBER				
M	T	W	Th	F

never

floor

1st 2nd 3rd 4th 5th 6th 7th 8th

behind

between

in front of

next to

Ordinal numbers

1 Read, label, and complete.

John is between Peter and Fred. Jane is in front of Jack. Sally is behind Fred. Lily is next to Peter. Jim is behind Jack. Vicky is in front of Lily.

1. Fred is ____*eighth*____ in line.
2. Jane is ______________ in line.
3. Jack is ______________ in line.
4. Jim is ______________ in line.
5. John is ______________ in line.
6. Lily is ______________ in line.
7. Peter is ______________ in line.
8. Sally is ______________ in line.
9. Vicky is ______________ in line.

2 Look, read, and write.

1. Mr. James can swim in the pool near his apartment.
   He lives on the first floor.

2. There is a restaurant on Mr. Nakamura's floor.
   ______________________________.

3. Mr. Fontaine's apartment is the biggest of all.
   ______________________________.

4. Ms. Ramirez can exercise on the floor where she lives.
   ______________________________.

5. There are six apartments on Mrs. Giordano's floor.
   ______________________________.

6. There is a painting next to Mr. Simpson's apartment.
   ______________________________.

7. There is an apartment for sale on Ms. Yang's floor.
   ______________________________.

How often...? 1

1 Look, read, and circle.

Miss Amanda			Weekly planner: Class 3A		
Activities:	Monday	Tuesday	Wednesday	Thursday	Friday
being outdoors	X	X	X	X	
homework	X	X	X	X	X
exam	X				
new song		X		X	
new grammar	X		X		X

1. How often does Miss Amanda give exams?
   a. At four o'clock. b. Once a week. c. Every day.
2. How often does Miss Amanda teach new songs?
   a. On Wednesdays. b. She doesn't. c. Twice a week.
3. How often does Miss Amanda teach new grammar?
   a. Three times a week. b. Twice a week. c. Once a week.
4. How often does Miss Amanda give homework?
   a. Twice a week. b. Once a week. c. Every day.
5. How often does Miss Amanda do outdoor activities with her students?
   a. Twice a week. b. Once a week. c. Four times a week.

1 Read and sort.

I never go to bed late.

I always throw papers on the floor.

I never clean my room.

I always do my homework.

I always fix my friends' toys.

I never help my brother.

I never drink soda.

I always draw on the walls.

Good habits

I never go to bed late. ______

______

______

______

______

Bad habits

______

______

______

______

______

Sometimes, usually

1 Follow, read, and write.

1. *He usually buys a new car* __________ in spring.
2. ____________________ in the afternoon.
3. ____________________ in winter.
4. ____________________ on Fridays.
5. ____________________ in the morning.
6. ____________________ for lunch.

2 Read and circle.

Quiz: How healthy are you?

1. Do you eat fruit every morning?	never	sometimes	usually	always
2. Do you eat vegetables with your meals?	never	sometimes	usually	always
3. Do you exercise?	never	sometimes	usually	always
4. Do you go to bed early?	never	sometimes	usually	always
5. Do you drink six glasses of water every day?	never	sometimes	usually	always
6. Do you feel happy?	never	sometimes	usually	always
7. Do you smile?	never	sometimes	usually	always
8. Do you take a shower every day?	never	sometimes	usually	always
9. Do you brush your teeth after every meal?	never	sometimes	usually	always
10. Do you wash your hands after you go to the bathroom?	never	sometimes	usually	always

Mostly **never**: You really are very unhealthy. It's time for a change!

Mostly **sometimes**: You are healthy, but you could do better. Try harder!

Mostly **usually**: Well done! You take care of yourself. That's great!

Mostly **always**: Wow! You are amazingly healthy! Good job!

3 Look and write.

1 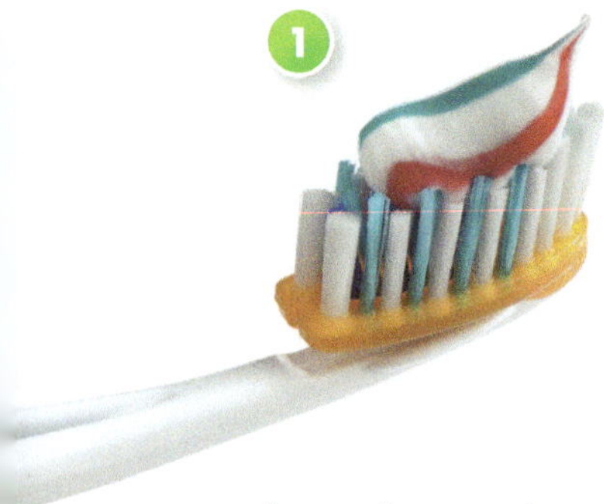

2 

3 

4 

5 

1. *I always brush my teeth twice a day*________.
2. ________________________________.
3. ________________________________.
4. ________________________________.
5. ________________________________.

4 Look, read, and write.

eat breakfast	eat lunch	get up	go to the library	walk to school	play basketball

1. Mary always *gets up* ______ at 7 o'clock.

2. She usually ______________ in the kitchen.

3. She always __________________ at 8:30.

4. She usually ____________ with her friends.

5. After school, she sometimes ____________ ______________________________________.

6. She always _________________________ with her friend at 5 o'clock.

1 Listen and write. 2

JACK: ___What___ do you do on the ________?

DAISY: I ____________________ with my friends.

________ we ________ a 3-D ________!

JACK: That sounds ________! ____________

do you ________ a 3-D ________?

DAISY: About ________ a ________.

2 Read the dialogue with a friend.

3 Talk with a friend. Then write.

A: ________, what do you do after school?

B: I usually ____________________.

Sometimes I ____________________.

A: That sounds fun! How often do you ____________________?

B: About ____________________.

Let's sing!

1 Listen and match. 3

French

Chinese

Japanese

English

Dutch

Mexican

Waiting in Line

Chorus:
Waiting in line
To see new lands
First, second, third,
And fourth we stand.

The Mexican boy is sixth in line.
It looks like he's having a good time.
The English girl is fifth; she looks sad,
Waving good-bye to her mom and dad.

The Dutch boy and girl are third and fourth
They are wearing coats; they're flying north.
Seventh in line speaks perfect Chinese.
He's saying that he doesn't like cheese.

The ninth and twelfth are both Japanese.
They're wearing green shorts above their knees
The eleventh left a note in French:
"My feet hurt; I'm sitting on the bench."

Unit 2

bath

businessman, businesswoman

celebrate (*v*)

chef

doctor

firefighter

fire station

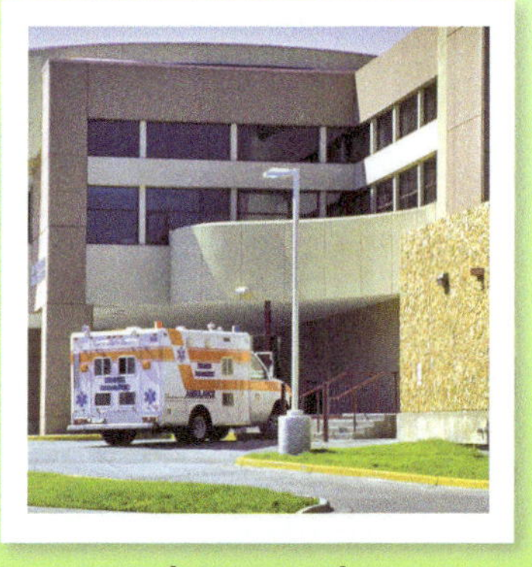
hospital

library

nurse

office

police officer

police station

restaurant

scientist

secretary

What does she do? 4

1 Match and write.

1. What ___does___ he ___do___?
   ___He's a nurse___.
2. What ______ she ______?
   ______ scientist.
3. ______?
   ______.
4. ______?
   ______.
5. ______?
   ______.
6. ______?
   ______.

Where do you work?

1 Match and write. Use colors.

1. Where does Sue work? *She works at a police station*.
2. Where *does* Bill *work*? *He works* ________.
3. ________? ________.
4. ________? ________.
5. ________? ________.

Why do you like your job?

1 Read, look, and write.

a. Because it's creative. b. Because I love food. c. Because I love water.
d. Because I can read all day. e. Because I make a lot of money.

1

2

3

4

5

When...?

1 Read, write, and match.

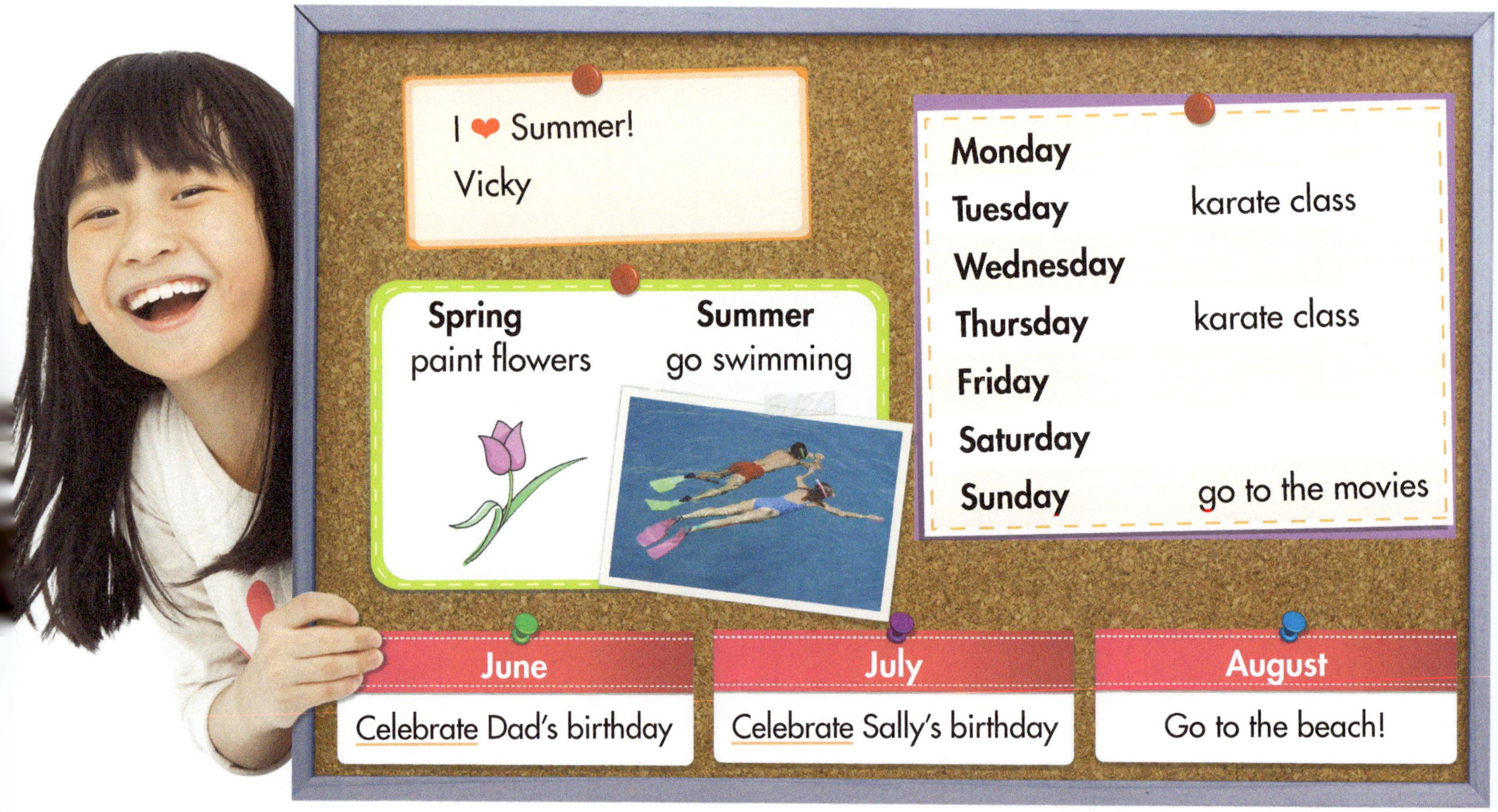

1. *When does* ______ Vicky paint flowers?
2. ______________ she go swimming?
3. ______________________ birthday?
4. ______________ she go to the movies?
5. ______________ have karate classes?
6. ______________________________?

In July.
On Tuesdays and Thursdays.
On Sundays.
In the summer.
In August.
In the spring.

Simple present vs. present continuous

1 Read, look, and write.

1. *travel / fly*

Jim doesn't usually ___travel___ by plane, but this year he ___is___ ___flying___ to Europe.

2. *celebrate / have*

Grace never ________________ her birthday, but this year she ________ ________________ a party.

3. *cook / buy*

Peter usually ________________ dinner, but today he ________________ pizza.

4. *drive / walk*

Jane usually ________________ to work, but today she ________________.

2 Match.

1. Where does he usually go on vacation?
2. When do they usually take their dog to the park?
3. What do you usually do for Christmas?
4. When does it usually rain in Mexico?
5. How often does she visit her grandma?

a. I usually stay at home, but this year I'm going to the beach.
b. She usually visits her twice a month, but this month she is going every day.
c. He usually goes to the mountains, but this year he's going to New York.
d. They usually take it there on Sundays, but this week they're taking it on Saturday.
e. It usually rains in the summer, but this year it's raining in the winter, too.

3 Read and answer.

1. Where do you usually go on weekends? I go *to the park* ______.
2. What are your friends doing now? ______
______.
3. Why are you studying English? ______
______.
4. How often does your teacher give exams? ______
______.
5. When do you usually go on vacation? ______
______.

4 Read, number, and unscramble.

1. Why does the secretary like her job?
   to answer / likes / the phone / she / Because
   *Because she likes to answer the phone*________.
2. Why does the police officer like his job?
   likes / to protect / Because / he / people
   ____.
3. Why does the scientist like her job?
   to learn / she / things / Because / likes / new
   ____.
4. Why does the businessman like his job?
   Because / likes / money / he / to make
   ____.

5 Read, look, and write.

Jenny and Mike usually go to  *school* on Fridays, but today they are staying at  ____________. Jenny is blowing up  ____________. Mike is making a  ____________. Their family doesn't usually celebrate birthdays, but today they are having a  ____________ because Great grandpa is 100 years old!

Let's talk!

1 Look, listen, and write. 5

NICK: Is Brian a *firefighter* ?

JILL: __________ so. He's wearing a __________ uniform.

NICK: You're ________! What about Keera? Is ____________?

JILL: I __________ so. She's wearing a ______________.

NICK: __________. Maybe she's a ________ or a ________!

Brian | Keera | Ben | Adam | Matt | Lucy

2 Read the dialogue with a friend.

3 Look again. Talk with a friend. Then write.

A: Is __________ a __________?

B: I (don't) think so. She's / He's ________________ uniform.

A: You're right. What about __________? Is __________ a __________?

B: I (don't) think so. She's / He's ________________.

A: You're right!

Let's sing!

1 Listen, read, and mark (✓). 6

The Job Song

What do you do? What do you do?
And where do you work?
At an office or a hospital,
At a bank or in a restaurant?

MS. WHITE:
I'm Ms. White and I work
At the fire station.
I always work and I get dirty,
So I'm taking a nice bath!

What do you do? What do you do?
Do you like your job?
Are you happy? Is your work okay?
Why do you like your job? Tell me!

MR. BLACK:
I'm Mr. Black, nice to meet you.
I work at a school.
Now I'm eating a chocolate snack.
I like my job 'cause I like children!

What do you do? What do you do?
And where do you work?

CHILDREN:
We are students and we go to school!
And we like our jobs a lot!

Meet Ms. White and Mr. Black

1 

- [x] Ms. White
- [ ] Mr. Black

2 

- [ ] Ms. White
- [ ] Mr. Black

3 

- [ ] Ms. White
- [ ] Mr. Black

4 

- [ ] Ms. White
- [ ] Mr. Black

Unit 3

bus station

bus stop

driver

ride (*n*, *v*)

ticket

bowl

cups

cheese

pasta

plate

salad

sandwich

soup

vegetables

Numbers 21–30

1 Connect in order.

21 twenty-one

28 twenty-eight

22 twenty-two

29 twenty-nine

27 twenty-seven

30 thirty

26 twenty-six

23 twenty-three

25 twenty-five

24 twenty-four

2 Count and write.

bowls cups plates

1. 

twenty-five cups

2. 

____

3. 

____

How many...? 7

1 Count, write, and circle.

bus station | hospital | bus stop | park

1. How _many_ bus stations are there?
   There are _two bus stations_.
   There are a few. (circled) / ***There are a lot.***
2. How ______ bus stops ______?
   There are ______________.
   There are a few. / There are a lot.
3. ______ parks ______?
   ______________.
   There are a few. / There are a lot.
4. ______ hospitals ______?
   ______________.
   There are a few. / There are a lot.

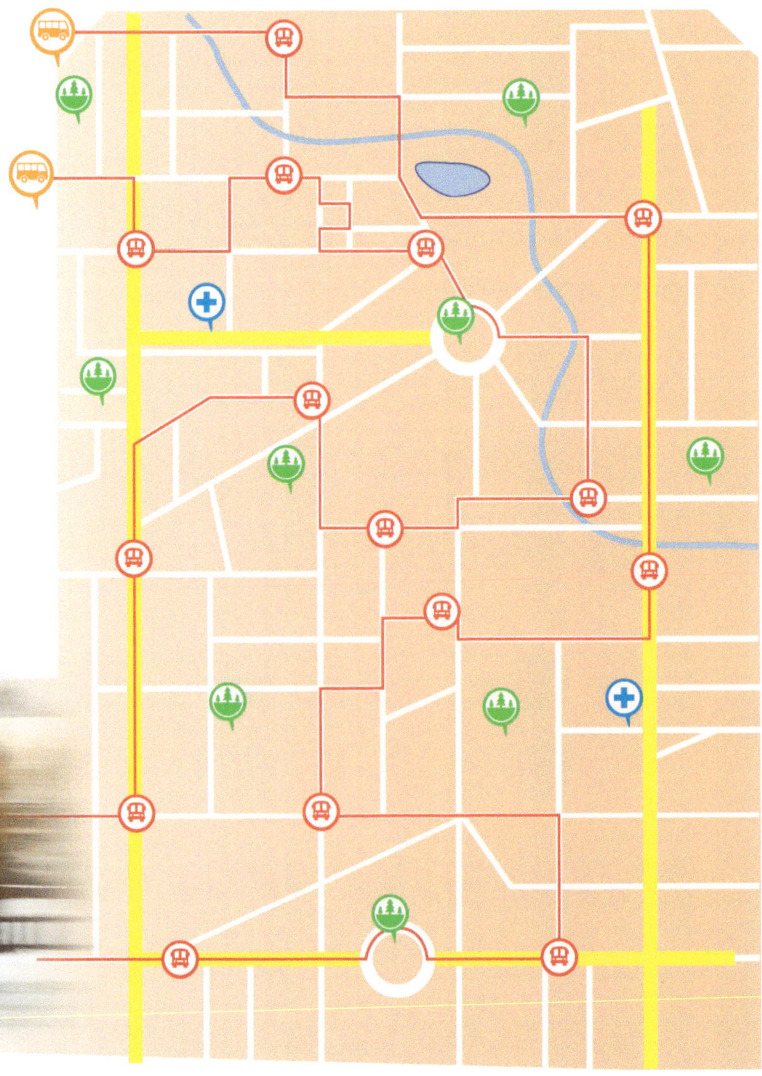

How much...?

1 Look and write.

1. ___How much___ cheese is there?

There is ___a lot of___ cheese!

There is ___a little___ cheese!

2. ______________ salad is there?

There is ______________ salad!

There is ______________ salad!

3. ______________________________?

______________ soup!

______________ soup!

Adjective word order

1 Sort.

American big blue British Chilean gray Mexican modern
new old purple rectangular red round small square

Size →	Age →	Shape →	Color →	Origin
big	______	______	______	*American*
______	______	______	______	______
	______	______	______	______
			______	______

2 Match and write.

1 Anna likes	big	black and white	French	bus ticket.
2 Dad is watching an	old	modern	purple	movie.
3 I am holding a	small	rectangular	Japanese	cars.

1. *Anna likes small, modern, Japanese cars*.
2. ______.
3. ______.

3 Write, circle, and draw. Use colors.

1. *size* *color* *origin*
   (a) / an ___small___, ___red___ ___Italian___ car
2. *size* *shape*
   a / an __________, __________ truck
3. *size* *age* *origin*
   a / an __________, __________ __________ cheese
4. *size* *color*
   a / an __________, __________ salad
5. *age* *color*
   a / an __________, __________ bus
6. *size* *age*
   a / an __________, __________ plate

1

2

3

4

5

6

4 Look and write.

1. *How much* ______ fruit salad is there? There is *a lot of fruit salad* ______.
2. ______ plates are there? There are *four plates* ______.
3. ______? ______.
4. ______? ______.
5. ______? ______.
6. ______? ______.

5 Match and write.

seven*teen*	27	thir______	15
______-three	______-five	17	______-seven
25	13	fif______	23

6 Look, circle, and write.

Luigi's Gigantic Italian Restaurant

Spaghetti with meatballs

1

Italian salad

2

Sandwich and soup

3

1. How ***many*** / ***much*** pasta is on the plate? There is a lot of pasta_______________.
2. How ***many*** / ***much*** meatballs are on the pasta? _______________.
3. How ***many*** / ***much*** vegetables are in the salad? _______________.
4. How ***many*** / ***much*** salad is in the bowl? _______________.
5. How ***many*** / ***much*** soup is there? _______________.
6. How ***many*** / ***much*** sandwiches are there? _______________.

7 Write, circle, and draw.

1. There is ***a little*** / ***a lot of*** _______________.
2. There are ***a few*** / ***a lot of*** _______________.

My ________ ________ Restaurant

Let's talk!

1 Listen and write. 8

DAISY: We're *traveling* ________ from the city ______________ to the airport.
How __________ does a __________ cost?

DRIVER: It __________, or two __________ for __________.

DAISY: Okay. How ______________ can I get for ______________?

DRIVER: You can get ______________.

DAISY: Great! ______________, please.

2 Read the dialogue with a friend.

3 Talk with a friend. Then write.

A: I'm traveling from __________ to __________.
How much does a bus ticket cost?

B: It costs __________, or __________ rides for __________.

A: How many rides can I get for __________?

B: You can get __________ rides.

A: Great! __________ tickets, please.

Did you practice with the Pathway to Certification app?

Let's sing!

1 Draw.

bike

boat

bus

car

plane

train

US truck
UK lorry

2 Listen and write. 9

More and More Wheels

Two wheels, four wheels, five wheels or more,
They all can take you from door to door.

The yellow ____________ is above my head,
It's six o'clock and you can hear the ____________ pass.
I hear the ____________ bell ring; it's shiny and red.
The ____________ is going underground very fast.

There are some people on a ____________ up in the sky.
There are many lights on a ____________ far in the sea.
The ____________ makes a lot of noise when it travels by.
The kids on the ____________ are waving to you and me.

Unit 4

cloudy (*adj*)

cold (*adj*)

hot (*adj*)

rain (*v, n*)

snow (*v, n*)

sunny (*adj*)

windy (*adj*)

boat (*n*)

go fishing (*v*)

outer space (*n*)

potatoes (*n*)

race (*n*)

table tennis (*n*)

bored (*adj*)

What's the weather like?

1 Label, write, and match.

sunny

____

____

Weather symbols

1. What's the weather like?
   It's sunny.
2. What's the weather ______?
   ______ cloudy.
3. What's the ______ like?
   ______ raining.
4. What's ______ like?
   ______ windy.
5. What's ______?
   ______ cold.
6. ______?
   ______ hot.
7. ______?
   ______ snowing.

____

____

____

____

2 Look and write.

1

Is it ______ sunny?

No, *it isn't* ______.

It's *raining* ______.

2

______ windy?

No, ______.

It's ______.

3

______ sunny?

______.

______.

4

______ hot?

______.

______.

3 Write and draw.

1. *Imagine it's June.*

   What's the ______ like?

   It's ______ *raining* ______.

   I'm wearing ______ *jeans* ______ and

   ______.

2. *Imagine it's November.*

   What's ______?

   It's ______.

   I'm wearing ______ and

   ______.

1

2

Practice with the Pathway to Certification app!

Going to, affirmative

1 Look and write.

1. My cousin Jimmy *'s going to drive* a truck.
2. My brothers ________________ for a famous team.
3. My cousin Julia ________________ with the Bolshoi Ballet.
4. I ________________ to outer space.
5. My friend Max ________________ houses.
6. My friends Ann and Lucy ________________ help old people.

Going to, negative

She **isn't going to** call.

She's going to call!

1 Choose, circle, and write.

1. Mollie isn't going to *wear the purple dress*_______________.
2. She isn't __________________________________.
3. ____.

4. Dan ______________________________________.
5. ____.
6. ____.

Going to, interrogative 35

1 Write, look, and match.

1. *drink milk*
   __*Are*__ you *going to drink milk*____?
2. *write an e-mail*
   ______ he ____________________?
3. *walk the dog*
   ______ we ____________________?
4. *play tennis*
   ______ he ____________________?
5. *go shopping*
   ______ she ____________________?
6. *swim*
   ______ they ____________________?

Yes, he is.

Yes, I am.

No, they aren't.

No, we aren't.

No, he isn't.

Yes, she is.

2 Read, complete, and write.

	Ben's weekly planner				
	Monday	Tuesday	Wednesday	Thursday	Friday
a.m.	get to school early	take a math exam	________ ________ ________		run a race
p.m.		________ ________ ________	have a piano lesson	watch a movie	

1. *Is Ben going to* ________ get to school early on Monday morning? Yes, *he is* ________.
2. Is he ________________ on Tuesday morning? Yes, ________.
3. ________________ have a piano lesson ________________? No, ________.
4. ________________ play table tennis ________________? No, ________.
5. ________________________________? ________.
6. ________________________________? ________.

3 Unscramble and write about next weekend.

1. going to / you / your bike / ride / are

   Are you going to ride your bike ________? ________.
2. eat / you / hamburgers / going to / are

   ________________________________? ________.
3. going to / have / a party / you / are

   ________________________________? ________.
4. are / watch / going to / you / a movie on TV

   ________________________________? ________.

Going to, question words

1 Read and complete.

1. What is she going to eat? — Potatoes.
2. ________ is he going to live? — In Paris.
3. ________ are they going to travel? — Tomorrow.
4. ________ are they going to get there? — By boat.
5. ________ are you going to wear? — Shorts.
6. ________ am I going to wear shorts? — Because it's hot.

Why
When
How
Where
What

2 Sort and write.

Why?
Because I like it.
____
____

To Tokyo.
In India.
By car.
Next week.
Water.

Where?
____
____
____

A pilot.
Because I like it.
Tomorrow morning.

What?
____
____
____

Soccer.
Because she's sick.

How?
____
____
____

When?
____
____
____

At home.
On foot.
By plane.
Because it's fun.
On Thursday.

Let's talk!

1 Listen and circle. 11

DAN: Pat, I'm bored. Shall we ***play*** / ***playing*** football?

PAT: No, it's hot. How about ***go*** / ***going*** swimming?

DAN: Yes, let's ***go*** / ***going*** swimming! Mum, can we ***go*** / ***going*** swimming?

2 Read the dialogue with a friend.

3 Talk with a friend. Then write.

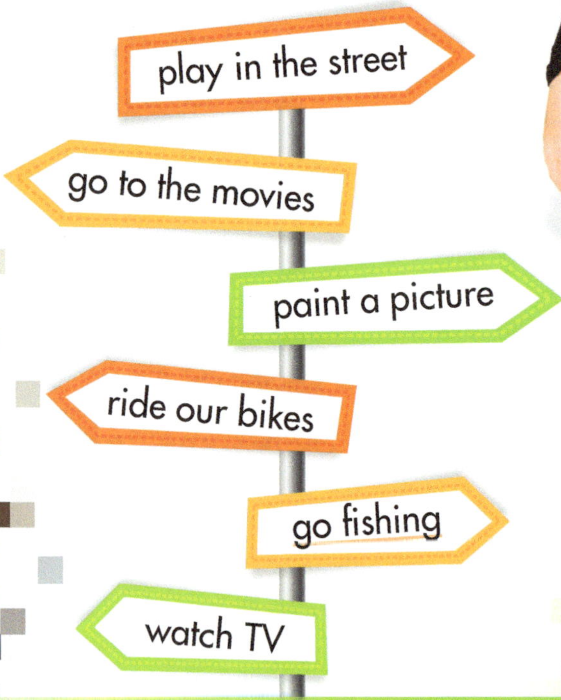

A: ____________, I'm bored.
Let's ____________!

B: No, it's ____________.
How about ____________?

A: Yes, let's ____________!
Mom, can we ____________?

Let's sing!

1 Complete. Then, listen and check. 12

Let's Sing about the Weather

Let's sing about the weather.

It's  __________ out and there's  __________.

My sister and I are going out. It's fun to play, you know.

Let's sing about the weather.

It's  __________ and it's wet.

It's time to play some video games with my best friend Ted.

Let's sing about the weather.

It's  __________ and it's  __________.

We are all traveling on the bus to our vacation spot!

2 Draw your favorite scene from the song.

Unit 5

bank

behind (*prep*)

bookstore

café

map

movie theater, theater

museum

near (*prep*)

opposite (*prep*)

shopping center

sports center

supermarket

swimming pool

Telling time, affirmative 13

1 Match.

1

It's four fifty-five.

3

It's ten twenty-one.

It's six thirty.

2

It's twelve oh eight.

4

2 Look and write.

1

What time is it?

It's seven fifty-one.

2

______________________________?

______________________________.

3
______________________________ in New York?

It's ______________________________.

New York

London

______________________________ in London?

______________________________.

Telling time, negative

Oops. It **isn't** 7:30. It's only 6:45.

It **isn't** 7:30. It's already 8:00!

1 Look and circle.

1

It's / ***It isn't*** seven eleven.

It's / ***It isn't*** seven twelve.

2

It's / ***It isn't*** two forty-four.

It's / ***It isn't*** four forty-two.

2 Look and write.

1

It isn't *one forty-four* ________.

It's *twelve forty-four* ________.

2

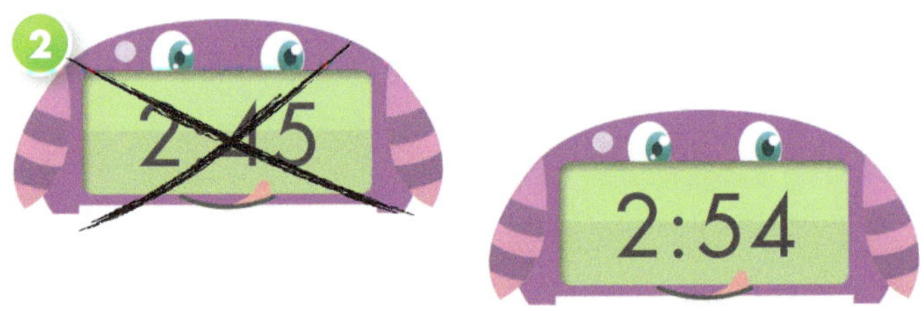

It isn't ________________.

It's ________________.

3

____________________.

It's ________________.

4

____________________.

It's ________________.

To be, past affirmative

1 Look and match. Then write.

sports center | movie theater | bank | supermarket

1. I *was at the bank last Sunday*.
2. They ______.
3. He ______.
4. We ______.

2 Circle. Then, write and draw a place.

I ***was*** / ***were*** at ______ yesterday.

Hmm… It **wasn't** small before.
It was big!

Oh no! They **weren't** yellow.
They were white!

1 Look and write in negative and in affirmative.

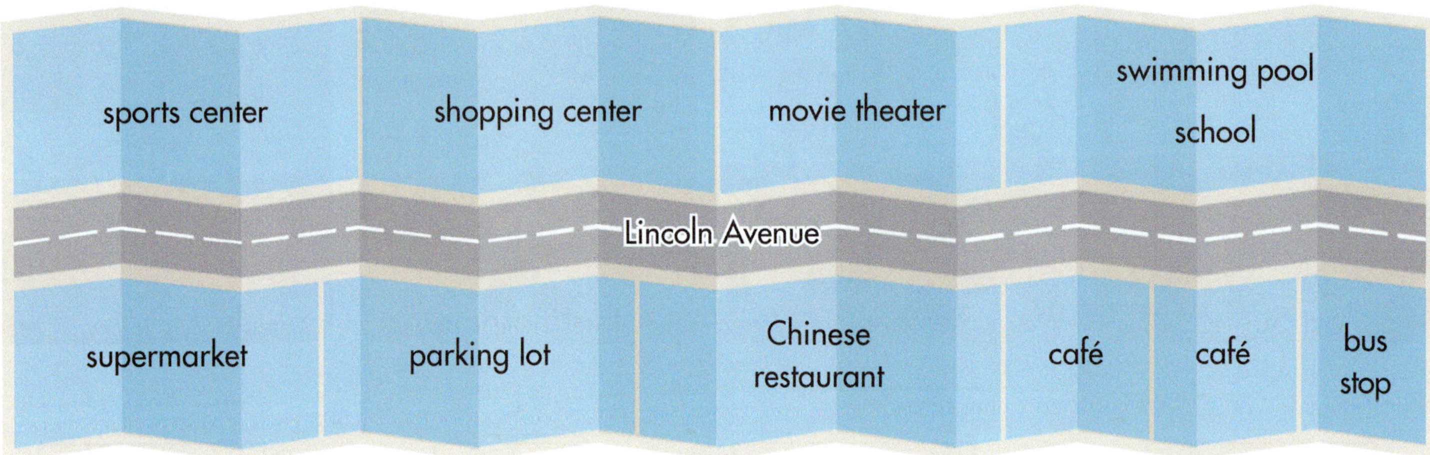

1. The swimming pool ___*wasn't*___ behind the sports center.
   It ___*was*___ behind the ___*school*___.
2. The supermarket __________ near the shopping center.
   It __________ near the ________________.
3. The cafés __________ opposite the movie theater.
   They __________ opposite the ________________.
4. The bus stop __________ next to the school.
   It __________ next to the ________________.

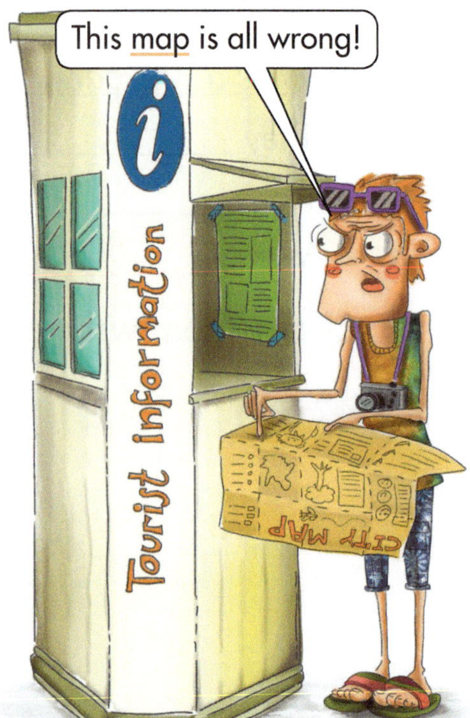

Practice with the Pathway to Certification app!

To be, past interrogative

1 Read and write.

was wasn't were weren't

Mike Brown: Last week, my sister Julie and I *weren't* in school because it _______ summer vacation. We _______ in Paris! It _______ boring. We _______ in a different place every day!

2 Write, look, and answer.

Mike Brown's Family Vacation

1. *Were* Mike and his family at the café on Wednesday? *No, they weren't*.
2. *Was* Mike at the museum on Monday and Tuesday? _______________.
3. ______ Julie and her mom at the market on Saturday? _______________.
4. ______ Mike at the shopping center on Sunday? _______________.
5. ______ Mike's dad at the bookstore on Thursday? _______________.
6. ______ the Browns at the park on Friday? _______________.

3 Look and write.

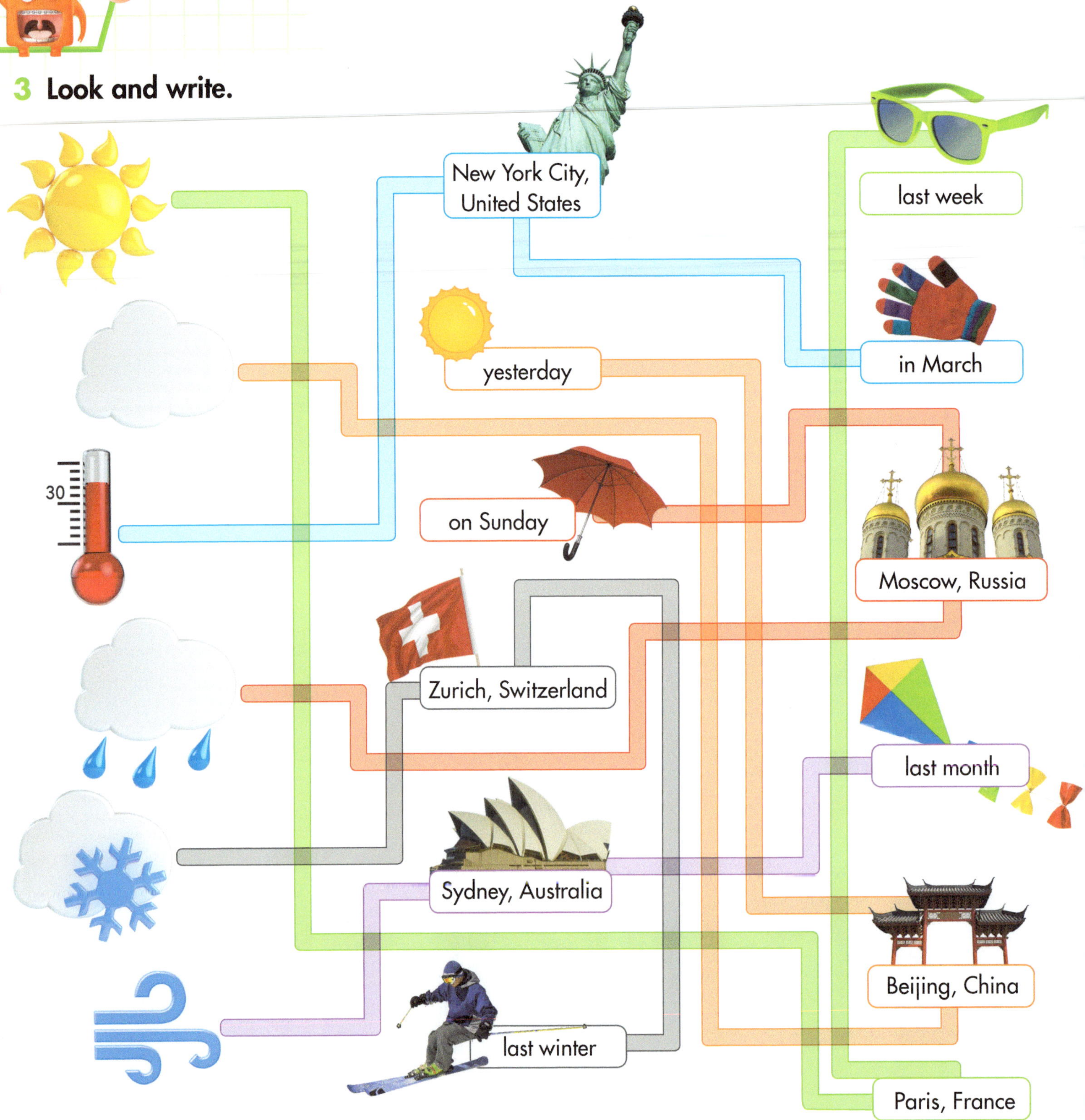

1. Was it *sunny in Paris* ______ last week? Yes, *it was* ______.
2. Was ______ in China yesterday? No, ______.
3. ______? ______.
4. ______? ______.
5. ______? ______.
6. ______? ______.

4 Unscramble and number.

1. were / They / the table / under

   They were under the table.

2. on / the chair / was / It

   ____________________________________.

3. and the table / between / was / It / the chair

   ____________________________________.

4. in / They / were / the box

   ____________________________________.

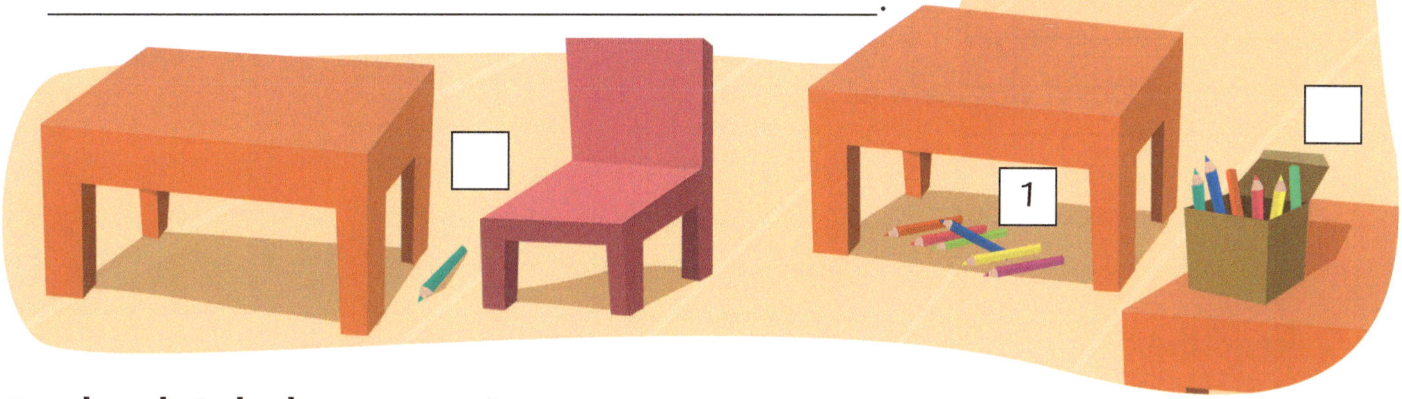

5 Read and circle the correct picture.

1. I wasn't old then.

2. We weren't happy last night.

3. The tree wasn't green in the fall.

4. They weren't big last year.

1 Listen and write. 14

EMILY: __How__ was the surprise party?

ALEX: It was terrible!

EMILY: Oh. ________ was it?

ALEX: Last Saturday night.

EMILY: ________ was it?

ALEX: At David's house.

EMILY: ________ wasn't it fun?

ALEX: Because the party was at ________,
but David was there at __________!
The food ________ on the table.
The decorations ________ ready.
So there ________ a surprise!

2 Read the dialogue with a friend.

3 Talk with a friend. Then write.

A: When were you at a party?

B: ________________________.

A: Where was it?

B: ________________________.

A: How was it?

B: ________________________.

A: Why was it ________________?

B: Because ____________________.

Let's sing!

1 **Listen and mark (✓) or (✗).** 15

2 **Listen and write.**

Those Prepositions!

Behind or next to? In or at?
Those prepositions drive me mad!
Dad's ________ the bookstore.
Where is he?
________ that bookcase,
Can't you see?

Mom's ________ the café,
Where is she?
________ her best friend,
Drinking tea.
We're ________ the classroom.
In or at?
Those prepositions drive us mad!

Unit 6

bring (*v*)

buy (*v*)

catch (*v*)

throw (*v*)

city (*n*)

clean (*v*)

countryside (*n*)

fall (*v*)

give (*v*)

go dancing (*v*)

go sailing (*v*)

go shopping (*v*)

go swimming (*v*)

go walking (*v*)

pirate (*n*)

presents (*n*)

Simple past, regular verbs 16

1 Look and write. Then number.

clean jump kick listen paint play talk watch

What We Did Yesterday

1

1. Amy _jumped_ rope.
2. Erin ________ a soccer ball.
3. Anika ________ to music.
4. Julie ________ television.
5. Ben ________ the car.
6. Eric ________ a picture.
7. Derek ________ on the phone.
8. Jamal ________ the trumpet.

Simple past, irregular verbs

1 Look, follow, and write.

ride

go

have

fly

fall

said | went | rode | gave | bought | swam | had | flew | got | fell

say

swim

get

buy

give

On Sunday Fred and Elsa _rode_ their bikes to the park. Their dog, Oliver, ______ with them. They ______ their kite, too. In the park, they ______ the kite for a long time. Suddenly, the kite ______ into the pond. "Oh, no!" Fred and Elsa ______. But then Oliver ______ into the water and ______ the kite. The kids were very happy. They ______ Oliver a big bone and ______ it to him on the way home. Then Oliver was very happy, too!

2 Sort.

Present				Past
eat	eat	see	made	*ate*
________	slept	brought	drank	________
________	wore	bring	make	________
________	saw	drink	ate	________
________	wear	sleep		________
________				________
________				________

3 Read and write.

Camp Royal
BEST FOR YOU

City Camp Schedule

Monday	go shopping
Tuesday	visit a museum
Wednesday	go walking in the park
Thursday	make bracelets
Friday	go dancing

Adventure
CAMPING TREKKING

Countryside Camp Schedule

Monday	fly kites
Tuesday	go fishing
Wednesday	go walking on the farm
Thursday	go swimming
Friday	sleep

Peter: My friend Lily and I went to camp last week.

1. I went to City Camp. On Monday, I *went shopping*.
2. Lily went to Countryside Camp. On Tuesday, she __________.
3. Last Thursday, the city campers __________ bracelets, and the countryside campers __________.
4. The city campers __________ last Friday, but the countryside campers __________ all night.
5. On Wednesday, all the campers __________.

Simple past, negative

1 Look, read, and mark (✓) or (✗).

1. [✗] We wore shoes on the beach.
2. [ ] My mom brought water.
3. [ ] My brother went sailing.
4. [ ] People walked on the beach.
5. [ ] The kite flew in the sky.
6. [ ] I ate a sandwich for lunch.
7. [ ] My sister went swimming.

2 Now, write the corrections to the incorrect sentences.

*We didn't wear shoes on the beach*____________________.

______________________________________.

______________________________________.

______________________________________.

Simple past, interrogative

1 Follow, look, and write.

1. *Did he go dancing* ? *Yes, he did* .
2. Did she ______ ? No, ______ .
3. ______ ? ______ .
4. ______ ? ______ .
5. ______ ? ______ .

2 Look and write.

buy eat give go shopping open walk

At ___ten thirty___, Sally ___went shopping___. She ________ a present for her friend Kim. She and her friend Amy ________ to Kim's house. At ________, they ________ Kim her birthday present. Kim ________ the present. At ________, they all ________ chocolate cake.

3 Circle, write, and draw.

1. This morning I (ate) / drank ___an apple___.

2. Last weekend I played / cleaned ________.

3. Yesterday I saw / wore ________.

4 **Unscramble, look, and circle.**

clown cowboy pirate

1. have / red / did / round / nose / a / you

   *Did you have a round, red nose?*_______________? No, I didn't.

2. brown / hair / did / have / you / short

   _______________________________? No, I didn't.

3. did / wear / hat / an / you / old / big

   _______________________________? Yes, I did.

4. your / black / hat / and / white / was

   _______________________________? No, it wasn't.

5. and / brown / hat / the / was / round

   _______________________________? Yes, it was!

5 **Now, look and circle.**

I know! You were a ***clown*** / ***cowboy*** / ***pirate*** !

6 **Draw and write.**

My Costume

1. I had _______________________________

   _______________________________.

2. I wore _______________________________

   _______________________________.

3. I _______________________________

   _______________________________.

Let's talk!

1 Listen and write. 17

GRANDMA: Hi, Michael! Why are you all by yourself?
MICHAEL: It's Saturday, Grandma. Everyone's busy!
GRANDMA: Where's your dad?
MICHAEL: He's at the _bank_. He went to ____________ money.
GRANDMA: Where's your mom?
MICHAEL: She's at the ______. She went to ____________.
GRANDMA: And where's your big sister?
MICHAEL: She's in the ______. She's cleaning ____________.
GRANDMA: And what about you?
MICHAEL: I went outside to ______ a nap!

2 Read the dialogue with a friend.

3 Talk with a friend. Then write.

Places	Actions
café	buy
library	eat
supermarket	drink
sports center	read
shopping center	play

A: Where's your ___________?
B: He's/She's at (the) ___________.
A: Oh. Why is he/she there?
B: He/She went to ____________________.
A: Where are your friends?
B: They're at ___________.
A: Why are they there?
B: They went to ___________.

Let's sing!

1 Listen and number. 18

1

The Captain's Adventures

1. My name is Captain Pollywog.
Last year I sailed with my dear dog,
In sun, in rain and in the fog,
Over the seven seas!
(Over the seven seas.)

2. A pirate threw us in the sea.
I saw a shark and it caught me.
I kicked its nose and I was free,
To swim the seven seas!
(And he swam in the sea.)

3. I saw an island with palm trees.
I lived there with the Balinese.
I said: "Take us to England, please,
Or to the seven seas!"
(Oh, take him to the sea!)

4. A ship took me to Istanbul,
To Paris and to Liverpool.
Now I can work or go to school,
But never to the seas!
(No, never back to sea!)

Unit 7

bat

climb (*v*)

dolphin

forest

kangaroo hop (*v*)

lion roar (*v*)

panda

parrots

rock

shark

skate,
ice skate (*v*)

take a picture (*v*)

think (*v*)

wake up (*v*)

whale

Past time expressions

1 Read and write.

________	Sunday:	________	________	Wednesday:
____ days ________	three days ago	the day ________ ________	yesterday	today

2 Read, look, and circle. Use colors.

1. six weeks ago
2. the day before yesterday
3. yesterday
4. last Tuesday
5. five days ago
6. last month

3 Look and write.

climb fly hop are jump see take think

Sunday, June 1st

Monday, June 2nd

Tuesday, June 3rd

Wednesday, June 4th

Thursday, June 5th

Friday, June 6th

Saturday, June 7th, Australia

1. Five ___days ago___, I ___saw___ a bat in the forest, but it ___flew___ away in the dark!
2. Last ______________, I _______ a picture of a parrot in a tree.
3. Four ______________, four kangaroos _______ in front of me!
4. The day ______________, I _______ on the tall rocks by the sea.
5. ______________ there _______ dolphins in the water.
   I ______________ they were sharks!
6. Three ______________, a whale _______ out of the water.
   It was amazing!

4 Write.

1. The day before yesterday, I ____.
2. One week ago, I ____.

Simple past, question words 19

1 Read and circle. Then number.

1. *What* / (*When*) did she *dance* / (*play*) tennis?
2. *Where* / *How* did you *see* / *fall* a panda on a rock?
3. *How* / *What* did they *go* / *fly* to the city?
4. *When* / *Why* did we *watch* / *walk* in the forest yesterday?
5. *How* / *What* did he *sing* / *celebrate*?
6. *Why* / *What* did the giraffes *hop* / *drink* water?

The day before yesterday.
In the zoo.
By bus.
Because it was beautiful.
His birthday.
Because they were hot.

1

2 Look, read, and write.

how what when where why

1. What did ______ the panda eat ______?
   It ate bamboo.
2. Where did ______ the dolphin swim ______?
   It swam in the big pool.
3. ______ the bat ______?
   It slept upside down.
4. ______ the parrots ______?
   They flew up to the top of the tree.
5. ______ the lions ______?
   They played because they were happy.
6. ______ the kangaroo ______ on the path?
   It hopped on the path two days ago.

3 Write.

1. What did you eat for lunch two days ago?
   Two days ago, I ate ______.
2. Where did you go last summer?
   ______.
3. How did you go to school yesterday?
   ______.

Could for past ability

1 Read, look, and circle.

I could paint when I was five.

I couldn't jump rope when I was seven.

I could fly when I was one.

1

2

3

2 Look and write *could* or *couldn't*.

1. The lion __________ roar when it was little.
2. The dolphin __________ swim when it was little.

Could for past ability, interrogative

1 Look, read, and write.

1 

Could you ride a bike ?

Yes, I could .

2 

__________ you swim ?

No, I couldn't .

3 

__________ you __________ ?

No, __________ .

4 

____________________ ?

Yes, __________ .

5 

____________________ ?

Yes, __________ .

6 

____________________ ?

No, __________ .

2 Write and draw.

1. When I was little, I could ______________________.

2. When I was little, I couldn't ______________________.

3 Answer with complete sentences.

1. When were you five years old?
   I was five years old ____________ *years ago*.
2. When you were five, could you ride a bike?
   ______________________.
3. How did you get to school then?
   ______________________.
4. Where did you go after school?
   ______________________.
5. What did you do there?
   ______________________.
6. Did you like it? Why?
   ____________, because ____________.

1 Listen and write. 20

VICKY: Where did you go ______________?
JOHN: I went to the __________.
VICKY: That's nice! __________ you see?
JOHN: I saw the pandas. They __________ so funny! One panda slept in a tree. He was a fat __________, and it was a really skinny tree! I wanted to __________, but I didn't.
VICKY: __________ not?
JOHN: I __________ want to wake him up! Then he started to __________ out of the __________, so he woke up after all. But he was fine. He just started to __________!

2 Read the dialogue with a friend.

3 Talk with a friend. Then write.

A: I saw a really funny parrot!
B: Cool! When did you see it?
A: ____________________.
B: What did it do?
A: It started to __________.
I wanted to __________.
B: What did you do?
A: I started to __________.

Let's sing!

1 Write. Then, listen and check. 21

Vacation Stories

Where did you go?
What did you see?
How did you get there?
Please, tell me.

First, I _________ (*get*) on a plane,
And _________ (*fly*) over the ocean.
Next, I landed in Spain,
I didn't use sun lotion.
Then I _________ (*get*) really burned,
Oh, a good lesson I _________ (learn).

First, I _________ (*take*) a fast boat,
To a tropical island.
Next, I _________ (*learn*) how to float,
I _________ (*play*) with the golden sand.
Then I _________ (*climb*) a big rock,
Left a flag made of my sock.

First, I _________ (*jump*) on a truck,
And _________ (*drive*) up a high mountain.
Next, I _________ (*find*) a fat duck,
Near the hotel fountain.
Then I _________ (*cook*) it with rice,
Oh, my! It was very nice!

Unit 8

Months of the Year

loudly (*adv*)

quietly (*adv*)

slowly (*adv*) quickly (*adv*)

curly (*adj*)

straight (*adj*)

granddaughter grandson

clap (*v*)

sandals

stairs

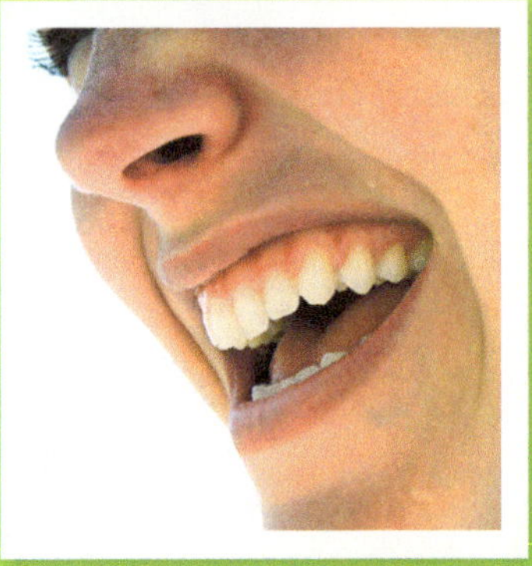

1 tooth, 2 teeth

Dates and years

1 Follow and write.

1. 1800 (eighteen)
2. 1900 (nineteen)
3. 2000 (two thousand)
4. 2000 (twenty)

45 14 99 3

1. _1899_ _eighteen ninety-nine_
2. ______ ______________________
3. ______ ______________________
4. ______ ______________________

2 Match, complete, and write.

Valentine's Day	Christmas Day	Halloween	New Year's Eve	Mother's Day
May 11	February 14	October 31	December 25	December 31

1. Valentine's Day is on _February 14th_.
2. Mother's Day is on ______________________.
3. Halloween is on ______________________.
4. Christmas Day is on ______________________.
5. New Year's Eve is on ______________________.

Punctuation

1 Match.

A — comma — ? — period

question mark — . — capital letter — ,

2 Sort and correct.

milk eggs and cheese | She has a grandson | Do you like it | ana

socks shoes and sandals | spain | I'm 11 years old | july

Does she read books | They climb the stairs | Did they clap | a cat a dog and a fish

Capital letter

____

____

____

Comma

milk, eggs, and cheese

____

____

Question mark

____

____

____

Period

____

____

____

3 Read, correct, and rewrite.

dear emily
here are some pictures of my
grandchildren! my granddaughter
anna has curly red hair like my son.
my granddaughter grace has
straight brown hair glasses and a big
smile. my grandson brian is just a
baby he doesn't have any teeth yet!
how are your grandchildren
love
pamela

Dear Emily,
___
___
___
___
___
___
___
___
___
___
___

4 Read and write.

1. *capital letter / comma / comma / period*
   I bought rice, milk, and bread.
2. *capital letter / capital letter / question mark*
   ___
3. *capital letter / comma / period*
   ___
4. *capital letter / comma / comma / question mark*
   ___

Subject pronouns 22

1 Match.

he	I	it	she	they	we	you

2 Circle.

1. ***They*** / ***I*** are from Mexico.
2. ***She*** / ***You*** has pink sandals.
3. ***It*** / ***She*** is my mother's new dress.
4. ***I*** / ***He*** am riding on a train.
5. ***He*** / ***We*** climbs the stairs at night.
6. ***It*** / ***You*** sleep late on weekends.

Object pronouns

1 Look, read, and write.

her   him   it   me   them   us   you

1 

They're monkeys. Don't feed _them_!

2 

It's a bat. Don't wake ______ up!

3 

She's little. Don't give ______ candy!

4 

He doesn't work at the zoo.
Don't buy bird food from ______!

5 

I'm talking, but you don't listen to ______!

6 

We're having fun. Don't take ______ home!

2 Look, read, and write.

1 

2 

3 

4 

1. He _caught_ _it_ in one hand.
2. He ________ ________ a Valentine's Day card.
3. They ________ ________ in thirty minutes.
4. I ________ ________ in Mom's closet.

3 Read and draw.

1 The teacher is asking us a question.

2 Mom is giving me a cookie.

3 We're calling him on the phone.

4 I'm talking to you.

4 Number, read, and write.

☐	December 21st, 1948	☐	August 17th, 1948
☐	October 13th, 2003	☐	December 11th, 1979
1	August 26th, 1910	☐	May 24th, 1937
☐	January 6th, 1929	☐	September 5th, 1997

Mother Teresa of Calcutta

Mother Teresa of Calcutta was born on August 26th, 1910, in Macedonia. Her real name was Gonxha Agnes Bojaxhiu. When she was 18 years old, she traveled to India. She arrived in Calcutta on ________________. There, she was a teacher. On ________________, she became a nun. On ________________, Mother Teresa put a white veil on her head. She wore a white and blue sari* and sandals. She started to work with poor people. On ________________, she went to the slums for the first time. She worked there for almost fifty years.

Mother Teresa won the Nobel Peace Prize on ________________. She died on ________________.

Because Mother Teresa helped thousands of people all over the world, Pope John Paul II canonized her on ________________.

* sari = Indian dress

A statue of Mother Teresa

Sisters of Mother Teresa's order in Cuba

5 Read and correct.

1. Mother Teresa was a nun. her real name was Gonxha.
2. She wore a white and blue sari a veil and sandals.
3. Mother teresa helped people in the slums of calcutta in India.
4. When did Pope John Paul II canonize her On October 13th 2003.

Let's talk!

1 Listen and write. 23

carefully loudly quietly quickly slowly

TEACHER: Class, let's play "Simon Says."
Remember, only do what Simon says!
Listen *carefully* ! Ready?
Simon says, "Clap!"
Simon says, "Clap ___________!"
Simon says, "Clap ___________!"
Simon says, "Clap ___________!"
Simon says, "Clap ___________!"
Now clap two times!
Did you clap two times? You're out!

2 Read the dialogue with a friend.

3 Talk with a friend. Then write.

clap run sing talk walk

A: Let's play "Simon Says!" Ready?
Simon says, "__________ quickly."
Simon says, "__________ slowly."
Now __________.

B: My turn! Simon says, "__________ loudly."
Now __________ quietly.
Simon says, "Listen carefully!"

Let's sing!

1 Listen and write. 24

Show Me Your Hands

Show _____ your hands,
Show _____ your two hands.
Move _____ up. Move _____ down. (2x)
And turn around!

Show me _____ ears,
Show me _____ two ears.
Pull _____ up. Pull _____ down. (2x)
And turn around! Turn around!

Now make a new song,
Make _____ new song.
Sing to _____. Sing it loud. (2x)
And _____ your _____,
And turn around. Turn around!

2 Now, write and sing.

Show me your ______________________________,
Show me your ______________________________.
____.
____. (2x)
And turn around! Turn around!

Grammar summary

Unit 1

Ordinal numbers							
1st	2nd	3rd	4th	5th	6th	7th	8th
first	second	third	fourth	fifth	sixth	seventh	eighth

How often...?				
How often	do	I you	sleep late? clean your room?	
	does	he she it	go outdoors?	Once a month. Three times a week. Every day.
	do	we you they	buy new books?	

Adverbs of frequency			
always 7 days a week	**usually** 4–6 days a week	**sometimes** 1–3 days a week	**never** 0 days a week

I always do my homework. I usually help my brother.

Unit 2

What do you do?				
What	do	you	do?	I'm a firefighter.
	does	he she		He's a businessman. She's a doctor.
	do	you they		We're chefs. They're police officers.

Why do you like your job?

Why	do	you	like	your	job?	Because I like helping people.
	does	he she		his her		Because he can read all day. Because she makes money.
	do	you they		your their		Because it's creative. Because they love food.

When...?

When	do	you	plant flowers?	In August.
	does	he she	pick potatoes?	On Tuesdays.
	do	you they	go to the market?	In the winter.

Simple present verbs, affirmative

I You	clean	the house.
He She It	cleans	
We You They	clean	

Simple present verbs, negative

I You	don't	clean the house.
He She It	doesn't	
We You They	don't	

Simple present verbs, interrogative

Do	I you	clean the house?	Yes, you do. / No, you don't. Yes, I do. / No, I don't.
Does	he she it	play basketball?	Yes, he does. / No, he doesn't. Yes, she does. / No, she doesn't. Yes, it does. / No, it doesn't.
Do	we you they	go to the park?	Yes, you do. / No, you don't. Yes, we do. / No, we don't. Yes, they do. / No, they don't.

Unit 3

How many...?

How many	ducks trees floors	are there?	There are a few ducks. There are a lot of trees. There are eight floors.

How much...?

How much	cheese bread	is there?	There is a little cheese. There is a lot of bread.

Adjective word order

size →	age →	shape →	color →	origin →
big small	old new	round square	red blue	British Italian

This is a tall, red, British bus.
This is the museum's big, new, square painting.

Unit 4

What's the weather like?

What's the weather like?	It's cloudy. It's raining. It's hot.

Going to, affirmative

I	am	(I'm)	going to	wear a purple shirt. go dancing. talk to the teacher.
You	are	(You're)		
He / She / It	is	(He's / She's / It's)		
We / You / They	are	(We're / You're / They're)		

Going to, negative					
I	am	not	(I'm not)	going to	do homework. write a letter. jump in the water.
You	are		(You aren't)		
He She It	is		(He isn't) (She isn't) (It isn't)		
We You They	are		(We aren't) (You aren't) (They aren't)		

Going to, interrogative				
Am	I	going to	listen to music? play soccer? walk the dog?	Yes, you are. / No, you're not.
Are	you			Yes, I am. / No, I'm not.
Is	he she it			Yes, he is. / No, he isn't. Yes, she is. / No, she isn't. Yes, it is. / No, it isn't.
Are	we you they			Yes, you are. / No, you aren't. Yes, we are. / No, we aren't. Yes, they are. / No, they aren't.

Going to, question words		
How	am I going to get there?	By train.
What	are you going to eat?	Pasta.
When	is he / she / it going to arrive?	Tomorrow.
Where	are we going to live?	In Rome.
Why	are they going to wear hats?	Because it's hot.

To be, past, affirmative		
I	was	at the pool last Tuesday.
You	were	near the café yesterday.
He She It	was	in Paris five years ago.
We You They	were	tired the day before yesterday.

To be, simple past, negative				
I	was	not	(I wasn't)	sad this morning.
You	were		(You weren't)	next to the movie theater.
He She It	was		(He wasn't) (She wasn't) (It wasn't)	opposite the town hall.
We You They	were		(We weren't) (You weren't) (They weren't)	at the hospital.

To be, past, interrogative			
Was	I	at the bank?	Yes, you were. / No, you weren't.
Were	you	in school?	Yes, I was. / No, I wasn't.
Was	he she it	happy?	Yes, he was. / No, he wasn't. Yes, she was. / No, she wasn't. Yes, it was. / No, it wasn't.
Were	we you they	on the phone?	Yes, you were. / No, you weren't. Yes, we were. / No, we weren't. Yes, they were. / No, they weren't.

What time is it?	
What time is it?	It's twelve o'clock. It's six thirty. It's eight twenty-two.

Unit 6

Simple past, affirmative

I You He / She It We You They	climbed a tree. cooked dinner. rained at night.

Simple past, negative

I You He / She It We You They	didn't	climb a tree. cook dinner. rain at night.

Simple past verbs (irregular)

bring	brought	make	made
buy	bought	ride	rode
catch	caught	say	said
drink	drank	see	saw
eat	ate	sleep	slept
fall	fell	swim	swam
fly	flew	take	took
get	got	think	thought
give	gave	throw	threw
go	went	wake up	woke up
have	had	wear	wore

Simple past, interrogative

Did	I	go dancing? skate on the ice? walk to school? hop three times?	Yes, you did. / No, you didn't.
	you		Yes, I did. / No, I didn't.
	he she it		Yes, he did. / No, he didn't. Yes, she did. / No, she didn't. Yes, it did. / No, it didn't.
	we you they		Yes, you did. / No, you didn't. Yes, we did. / No, we didn't. Yes, they did. / No, they didn't.

Unit 7

Question words with simple past		
How	did I wake up yesterday?	I woke up with an alarm clock.
What	did you say a minute ago?	I said, "Hello!"
When	did he / she / it sing?	He / She / It sang last night.
Where	did we eat last weekend?	We ate at a restaurant.
Why	did they go home last night?	Because it rained.

Could for past ability, affirmative, negative			
I	could couldn't	ride a bike. swim. drive a car. cook dinner.	when I was five.
You			three years ago.
He She It			when he was ten. when she was four. last year.
We You They			when we were six. when you were twelve. when they were little.

Could for past ability, interrogative			
Could	I	write? paint a picture? play the piano? jump rope?	Yes, you could. / No, you couldn't.
	you		Yes, I could. / No, I couldn't.
	he she it		Yes, he could. / No, he couldn't. Yes, she could. / No, she couldn't. Yes, it could. / No, it couldn't.
	we you they		Yes, you could. / No, you couldn't. Yes, we could. / No, we couldn't. Yes, they could. / No, they couldn't.

Unit 8

Dates and years	
I was born on June 10th, 2003.	I was born in 2001.

Punctuation

Periods and question marks

Could you read a book when you were four**?**

Mr**.** Banks went fishing and caught a large fish**.**

Capital letters

The letter was for **M**rs. **W**hite in **L**os **A**ngeles, **C**alifornia.

Commas

Mom bought bread**,** milk**,** and eggs at the store.

On August 1st**,** 1996**,** my sister was born.

Subject pronouns

I am washing the car.

You broke the vase.

He likes carrots.

She wants a new toy.

It is beautiful.

We went shopping.

You have a kitten.

They are playing basketball.

Object pronouns

My teacher gave **me** a pencil.

Alex is making **you** a birthday cake.

An alarm clock woke **him** up.

The boy throws the ball to **her**.

My brother broke **it**.

Mom drove **us** home in her car.

The girls are giving **you** a present.

We gave **them** ice cream after dinner.

Audio script

Unit 1

Track 1

BOY: Yum, chips and cookies for lunch!
GIRL: That's really unhealthy! How often do you eat junk food?
BOY: Once a month.
GIRL: Yum, apples and carrots!
BOY: How often do you eat fruits and vegetables?
GIRL: Sunday, Monday, Tuesday, Wednesday, Thursday, Friday, Saturday… Every day!

Track 2

BOY: What do you do on the weekend?
GIRL: I usually watch movies with my friends. Sometimes we see a 3-D movie!
BOY: That sounds fun! How often do you see a 3-D movie?
GIRL: About once a month.

Track 3
Waiting in Line
(See page 13.)

Unit 2

Track 4

WOMAN: So, what do you do?
MAN: I'm a scientist. And what do you do? (GASPS) Oops!
WOMAN: I'm a firefighter!

Track 5

BOY: Is Brian a firefighter?
GIRL: I think so. He's wearing a firefighter's uniform.
BOY: You're right! What about Keera? Is she a chef?
GIRL: I don't think so. She's wearing a different uniform.
BOY: You're right. Maybe she's a doctor or a scientist!

Track 6
The Job Song
(See page 23.)

Unit 3

Track 7
(See page 26.)

Track 8

WOMAN: We're traveling from the city bus station to the airport. How much does a bus ticket cost?
MAN: It costs six dollars, or two rides for ten dollars.
WOMAN: Okay. How many rides can I get for twenty dollars?
MAN: You can get four rides.
WOMAN: Great! Four tickets, please.

Track 9
More and More Wheels

(Chorus:)
Two wheels, four wheels, five wheels or more,
They all can take you from door to door.

The yellow helicopter is above my head,
It's six o'clock and you can hear the buses pass.
I hear the tram bell ring; it's shiny and red.
The metro is going underground very fast.

(Chorus)

There are some people on a plane up in the sky.
There are many lights on a ship far in the sea.
The truck makes a lot of noise when it travels by.
The kids on the train are waving to you and me.

(Chorus)

Unit 4

Track 10

BOY & GIRL: Hi, Grandma!
WOMAN: Hello, Dan! Hi, Grace!
BOY: Are you going to read us a story?
WOMAN: Sure, I…
GIRL: Are you going to make us a cake?
WOMAN: Well, I…
BOY: Are we going to go to the park?
GIRL: Are you going to play with us?
WOMAN: Goodbye, Dan. Goodbye, Grace.
BOY & GIRL: Oh, no!

Track 11

BOY: Pat, I'm bored! Shall we play football?
GIRL: No, it's hot. How about going swimming?
BOY: Yes, let's go swimming! Mum, can we go swimming?

Track 12

Let's Sing about the Weather

Let's sing about the weather.
It's cold out and there's snow.
My sister and I are going out.
It's fun to play, you know.

Let's sing about the weather.
It's raining and it's wet.
It's time to play some video games
With my best friend Ted.

Let's sing about the weather.
It's sunny and it's hot.
We are all traveling on the bus
To our vacation spot!

Unit 5

Track 13

BOY: Mom, what time is it?
MOM: It's six twenty-eight.
GIRL: What time is it now?
MOM: It's six twenty-nine.
BOY: And now…?
MOM: Shhhh!
ACTOR: Now, it's show time! Welcome to the theater!

Track 14

EMILY: How was the surprise party?
ALEX: It was terrible!
EMILY: Oh. When was it?
ALEX: Last Saturday night.
EMILY: Where was it?
ALEX: At David's house.
EMILY: Why wasn't it fun?
ALEX: Because the party was at six thirty, but David was there at six o'clock! The food wasn't on the table. The decorations weren't ready. So there wasn't a surprise!

Track 15

Those Prepositions!

Behind or next to? In or at?
Those prepositions drive me mad!
Dad's at the bookstore. Where is he?
Near that bookcase, can't you see?

Mom's at the café, where is she?
Next to her best friend, drinking tea.
We're in the classroom. In or at?
Those prepositions drive us mad!

Unit 6

Track 16

GIRL: "To Do List. Item 1: Clean your room." Hmm...
GIRL: Whew! Okay, Mom. I cleaned my room!
MOM: Great! Let's see...
MOM: Eek! Umm...
GIRL: Mom, you opened my closet door!

Track 17

GRANDMA: Hi, Michael! Why are you all by yourself?
MICHAEL: It's Saturday, Grandma. Everyone's busy!
GRANDMA: Where's your dad?
MICHAEL: He's at the bank. He went to get money.
GRANDMA: Where's your mom?
MICHAEL: She's at the store. She went to buy milk.
GRANDMA: And where's your big sister?
MICHAEL: She's in the house. She's cleaning her room.
GRANDMA: And what about you?
MICHAEL: I went outside to take a nap!

Track 18

The Captain's Adventures

My name is Captain Pollywog.
Last year I sailed with my dear dog,
In sun, in rain and in the fog,
Over the seven seas!
(Over the seven seas.)

A pirate threw us in the sea.
I saw a shark and it caught me.
I kicked its nose and I was free,
To swim the seven seas!
(And he swam in the sea.)

I saw an island with palm trees.
I lived there with the Balinese.
I said: "Take us to England, please,
Or to the seven seas!"
(Oh, take him to the sea!)

A ship took me to Istanbul,
To Paris and to Liverpool.
Now I can work or go to school,
But never to the seas!
(No, never back to sea!)

Unit 7

Track 19

ZOOKEEPER: ...and here are the lions!
BOY 1: Oh. They're all asleep!
ZOOKEEPER: Well, the lions are sleeping now. But last night, the lions woke up!
BOY 1: When did they wake up?
GIRL 1: Where did they go?
BOY 2: What did they do?
GIRL 2: How did they talk?
ZOOKEEPER: They ROARED!

Track 20

VICKY: Where did you go last Saturday?
JOHN: I went to the zoo.
VICKY: That's nice! What did you see?
JOHN: I saw the pandas. They were so funny! One panda slept in a tree. He was a fat panda, and it was a really skinny tree! I wanted to laugh, but I didn't.
VICKY: Why not?
JOHN: I didn't want to wake him up! Then he started to fall out of the tree, so he woke up after all. But he was fine. He just started to eat!

Track 21

Vacation Stories

(Chorus:)
Where did you go?
What did you see?
How did you get there?
Please, tell me.

First, I got on a plane,
And flew over the ocean.
Next, I landed in Spain,
I didn't use sun lotion.
Then I got really burned,
Oh, a good lesson I learned.

(Chorus)

First, I took a fast boat,
To a tropical island.
Next, I learned how to float,
I played with the golden sand.
Then I climbed a big rock,
Left a flag made of my sock.

First, I jumped on a truck,
And drove up a high mountain.
Next, I found a fat duck,

Near the hotel fountain.
Then I cooked it with rice,
Oh, my! It was very nice!

(Chorus)

Unit 8

Track 22
MOM: Oh, no, that was very expensive! All right, everyone. Who broke this vase?
BOY: He did.
BOY 2: She did.
GIRL: No, they did!
DAD: Okay, okay, I did. I broke the vase. I'm sorry!

Track 23
TEACHER: Class, let's play "Simon Says." Remember, only do what Simon says! Listen carefully! Ready?
Simon says, "Clap!"
Simon says, "Clap quickly!"
Simon says, "Clap slowly!"
Simon says, "Clap loudly!"
Simon says, "Clap quietly!"
Now, clap two times!
Did you clap two times? You're out!

Track 24
Show Me Your Hands
Show me your hands,
Show me your two hands.
Move them up. Move them down. (2x)
And turn around!

Show me your ears,
Show me your two ears.
Pull them up. Pull them down. (2x)
And turn around! Turn around!

Now make a new song,
Make your new song.
Sing to me. Sing it loud. (2x)
And clap your hands,
And turn around. Turn around!

Vocabulary